Read and Play
Planes

by Jim Pipe

Stargazer Books

plane

2

This is a **plane**.

A **plane** can fly.

3

wings

A plane
has **wings**.

4

Wings help a plane fly.

5

wheels

6

A plane has **wheels**.

Wheels roll along a runway.

7

engine

8

This plane has a jet **engine**.

propeller

This plane has a **propeller**.

9

pilot

10

This plane has two **pilots**.

A **pilot** flies a plane.

11

airport

This is an **airport**.

12

A plane lands at an **airport**.

13

jumbo

A **jumbo** is a big plane.

It carries lots of people.

short

This plane has **short** wings.

long

This plane has **long** wings.

17

sea

18 A **sea**-plane lands on water.

stunt

This plane does **stunts**.

19

What am I?

wheels

wing

pilot

engine

Match the words and pictures.

How many?

Can you count the planes?

21

Look up!

balloon

butterfly

helicopter

bird

Look in the sky. What else can fly?

Index

Can you find these
pictures of planes
in the book?

For Parents and Teachers

Questions you could ask:

p.2 What can you see in this picture? e.g. clouds in background. Many passenger planes fly high in the sky, above the clouds.

p. 4 What else has wings? e.g. flying animals such as birds, bees, and butterflies.

p. 6 Can you see the runway? A runway is a hard, smooth surface for the plane to land on. Ask: What if a plane landed on a soft or bumpy surface?

p. 8 Where are the engines on these planes? e.g. jet engine is on the wing, propeller engine is at front of plane. Spot engines on other planes in the book.

p. 10 Where do pilots sit? In the cockpit (usually at front). Point out cockpits on other planes in the book.

p. 12 What is happening in this picture? e.g. plane refueling and baggage being loaded. People get on to the plane using a walkway (see picture) or stairs.

p. 14 How big do you think this plane is? Compare the plane with the person standing on the runway.

p. 17 What is unusual about this plane? It does not have an engine. A glider has long wings to help it glide like a bird. Another plane pulls it into the air.

p. 18 What is different about these two planes? e.g. floats/wheels, number of wings, pilot inside/outside.

p. 20 What am I? If they need a clue, children can look back to pages 4, 6, 8, and 10.

Activities you could do:

• Ask the reader to draw a simple plane, writing labels for wings, engine, wheels, cockpit, cabin.

• Ask the reader to act out how a plane or bird moves through the sky. Encourage them to make the appropriate noises if they know them.

• Ask the reader to describe a flight they might like to go on, e.g. what happens at take-off.

• You could help the reader to fold paper into a dart to show how a glider flies.

• Build a plane mobile using plane shapes cut from cardboard and painted. Mobiles can be made using criss-cross straws tied with yarn or string.

© Aladdin Books Ltd 2007

Designed and produced by
Aladdin Books Ltd

All rights reserved

Printed in the United States

Series consultant
Zoe Stillwell is an experienced preschool teacher.

First published in 2007
in the United States
by Stargazer Books
c/o The Creative Company
123 South Broad Street
P.O. Box 227
Mankato, Minnesota 56002

Photocredits:
l-left, r-right, b-bottom, t-top, c-center, m-middle All photos from istockphoto.com except: 4-5, 23br — British Airways copyright images. 6-7 — US Navy. 10-11, 20br, 22tl & bl — Corbis. 14-15, 23bl – Airbus. 23br – Stockbyte. 22tr — Otto Rogge Photography.

Library of Congress Cataloging-in-Publication Data

Pipe, Jim, 1966-
    Planes / by Jim Pipe.
        p. cm. -- (Read and play)
    Includes Index.
    ISBN 978-1-59604-118-9
    1. Airplanes--Juvenile literature. I. Title.

TL547.P523 2006
629.133'34--dc22

2005055538